The Quatermass Experiment

and its Legacy.

By

Adrian Sherlock

The Quatermass Experiment

and its Legacy.

Foreword

Welcome to this Second Edition of The Quatermass Experiment and its Legacy. As a writer and journalist, I was very surprised and very pleased by the success of the first version of this piece which began life as a humble "short read " for the Kindle market.

I did get one comment, however, from a reader who felt it was all a little too short. With that in mind, I expanded upon the original draft. I also wrote a longer work on the topic of the sequel serial, Quatermass 2. I hadn't gotten around to Quatermass and the Pit, but I had commented upon it for another book I was putting together.

Then two things happened. Firstly, the other book came out and got a rather bad reception and secondly, I noticed that the piece on Q2 was not exactly taking off either. Finally, I decided to put together this Second Edition of Quatermass Experiment and its Legacy. I have added the full text of my work on Quatermass 2 as well as the section about Quatermass and the Pit from my other book.

I've pulled the other book and the Q2 book from Amazon and Kindle and instead I want to give fans of Quatermass a chance to read all my writings on the Quatermass serials in one tome. It seems we live in an age where the big buzzword is value. Even Quatermass himself mentions in Q2 that using his nuclear rocket to destroy alien invaders might give the tax paying public some "value " for their money!

And so, in that spirit, I am proud to present this expanded second edition with some added value.

I hope you enjoy it!

Adrian

2018.

The Quatermass Experiment

In the beginning...

Quatermass!

You just have to say the name and you can almost hear the incredible dramatic strains of Holst's "Mars, the Bringer of War" pounding and pulsing out of the television speakers, shaking your soul and awakening an atmosphere of both excitement and dread.

Close your eyes as you listen to "Mars" as played by a full orchestra and you will almost see in your mind's eye that black-and-white cathode ray screen of an old TV and the blurring, flickering image of the opening titles. In the very first Quatermass serial, it was the title The Quatermass Experiment and it looked as though a human finger had painted the words across a dark and stormy sky. For viewers of this brand new entertainment medium, this must have been striking stuff indeed and even today, we cannot help but feel a little of their thrill of excitement as we look back on it.

It was in the year 1953, just a number of months after the coronation of Queen Elizabeth had encouraged many of the people of Britain to go out and buy their first ever TV set, that a bold young staff writer named Nigel Kneale brought his amazing, unforgettable opus, The Quatermass Experiment, to the screens of the BBC.

According to the writer, no one at the BBC had any faith at all in his project, with the possible exception of the man who had commissioned it and writer-director Rudolph Cartier. At that time, television drama was regarded as "radio with pictures" or theatre on the screen at best.

According to Kneale, the radio era men who dominated the BBC at that time were an arrogant, closed-minded and rather set-in-their ways bunch of execs, the type of people who looked down upon him disdainfully, and when they were not being willfully obstructive, they could be simply unpleasant.

However, Nigel Kneale was a man of great wit and talent as well as being something of a visionary, often able to foresee the future in a way, thanks to his grasp of the notion that what can go wrong, probably will go wrong eventually.

To name but one example, his play The Year of the Sex Olympics predicted the rise of reality TV shows like Big Brother, Survivor and others with astonishing accuracy, simply because he saw how television could be perverted to meet the needs of our most voyeuristic tendencies.

Yet what he scripted as a shocking science fiction tale of a potential terrible future came to pass, with the line only being drawn at actually causing serious harm or death to those who are watched for entertainment in reality TV.

Rudolph Cartier, too, was a man of vision, a film maker with a determination to bring the techniques and scope of cinema and movie-making to television.

The writer and director both had firm new ideas about the potential of the television medium for meaningful and impressive entertainment and they were determined to prove that television could deliver drama on an epic scale with visuals and stories to rival those of the best in world cinema at that time.

And yet at the same time, Kneale's scripts set out to show that television could use its weekly, chapter-like format to develop themes and characters in a way that a movie or play could not, building up in a way only matched or outdone by a novel. With Quatermass Experiment declaring itself 'A Serial in Six Parts', Kneale was setting out to sustain viewership and develop plots over a month and a half. This meant instead of ' radio with pictures', television would become cinema in chapters, with longer, more complex plots and richer, more fully evolved characters.

One glance at the arc-driven style of modern dramas like The Sopranos or Breaking Bad and we can see how Kneale and Cartier's vision for the potential of television eventually played out, making it not only a medium to take seriously, but possibly the greatest artistic medium of them all.

But in 1953, TV was still a medium in its infancy, everything was untried, untested, so it all came with a major element of risk. Performing drama live, like a stage play, for camera to transmit, was daring stuff. The Quatermass Experiment was very much a television drama experiment, then, a daring test of the potential and capabilities of the medium itself. We can only imagine the heightened sense of 'first night nerves' everyone must have been feeling when those opening credits rolled and the cameras finally went live!

And it is fair to say that the experiment was a rousing success, too. In fact, audience research showed that the six episode serial held its audience over all six weeks of its broadcast and its audience was enormous. Legend has it that pubs and clubs across England were emptied of a Saturday night as people rushed home to turn on their TV set so as not to miss each new instalment of the serial, as each episode was broadcast live.

It was the water-cooler talking point of the day and the writer Kneale gained a reputation as a man who could tell a story in such a way that it stopped you dead in your tracks, a way that was completely arresting to the viewer. It was a skill he would continue to hone, too, culminating in Quatermass and the Pit which captured the imagination like nothing before it and few things since.

According to the popular claims surrounding the serial, one in three people living in England at the time watched the serial. Today, such viewing statistics would be unthinkable, but at the time, TV audiences had limited choices and when the BBC delivered something so groundbreaking, it had a seismic impact.

Unfortunately for those of us who were not around to witness the broadcast at the time, only the first two episodes of the serial were recorded onto film for posterity. Sadly, episodes 3,4,5 and six were broadcast live but never recorded in any way, shape or form and so anyone who did not see them at the time missed the chance to see them ever again.

The reason the episodes were not recorded are uncertain. One story goes that the people who had the task of recording the episodes onto film by shooting them off a flat monitor decided to go on strike. The story goes that they pulled this small scale industrial action to demand more money when they realised the BBC could make money selling the serial overseas, which was presumably the reason for the tele-recording effort being mounted in the first place.

An alternative explanation is that the BBC gave up on the plan to preserve the serial after viewing the first two filmed recordings and finding them too poor in quality for overseas sales. This second theory could be true as episode two suffers from dark lighting and at one point a mosquito lands on the monitor screen, appearing as a surreal intruder in the episode, flitting about and taking rather a lengthy time to finally buzz off.

There are other noticeable technical issues with the tele-recordings, too, but it is still a heart breaking tragedy for fans of cult TV science fiction, horror and suspense that we cannot see a full recording of the serial, however crude, because the first two episodes and the script seem to promise a gripping tale indeed!

In part one, we see a space mission gone wrong, as the British Experimental Rocket Group or BERG struggles to locate its missing space craft, the Quatermass Rocket, a nuclear powered craft launched by Professor Bernard Quatermass.

The episode ends with a cliffhanger which, those who recall seeing it claim, scared the daylights out of viewers, when the hatch opens and a figure in a space suit comes staggering out. Quatermass discovers the remaining crew men … have vanished!

The second surviving episode deals with the astronaut in hospital and tests slowly starting to convey the disturbing idea that the man may in fact be a monster from space in some human-like form, the minds of all three astronauts locked inside of it.

Whatever went wrong with the plan to record the serial in all its unnerving glory, the ratings were extremely impressive and the enormous success of the TV serial led to the BBC selling the script to the fledgling Hammer movie studio who, at the time, were busy making low-budget films about historical subjects.

Without informing Nigel Kneale, the BBC sent the scripts to Hammer who passed them to a director named Val Guest. Guest was reluctant at first, but when prompted by his wife to read the scripts, he became involved, shooting a documentary style or cinema-verite horror film which retained the core of the serial.

Sadly, the most notable change in the film was the loss of Kneale's ending, in which the Professor exorcises the alien through words and reason. The film's replacement was a rather Hollywood style solution in which the army simply helps Professor Quatermass to fry the monster with electricity.

But in spite of the changed ending, the movie of Kneale's story made bank for Hammer films at the box office. Guest's direction was both realistic and shocking, with many hard-hitting moments, depicting bodies melted and half-dissolved by the touch of the astronaut-turned-monster. It was also an intelligent film and featured a strong set of performances.

When the movie version of the serial became an unexpectedly enormous hit, at least in Hammer's terms, and made a lot of money at the American box office, albeit with the alternative title "The Creeping Unknown", Hammer changed direction.

They junked their planned next film project, which was to have focused on British history and the Round-heads, and instead embarked on a career of making horror movies. Hammer horror films would become as famous in their own way as the Professor who had helped to launch them on their horrific way. In fact, as Hammer bought up the rights to such grisly tales as Frankenstein and Dracula, actors like Christopher Lee and Peter Cushing would soon become world famous for playing the Count and the good doctor respectively.

The writer Kneale, already unhappy that the BBC had sold the film rights to Hammer without even speaking to him about it, not to mention the fact he had no involvement in the film version, subsequently turned down an offer from Hammer to have his heroic Professor Quatermass feature in another Hammer film called "X the Unknown."

Written by Jimmy Sangster, who later wrote a terrifying episode for the mid-1970s American series The Night Stalker, titled The Horror in the Heights, "X the Unknown" would have been an interesting, if perhaps not remarkable, addition to the Quatermass canon. It's the tale of a life force from deep below the Earth's surface which has a deadly destructive power when it comes up top. With Kneale's refusal to get on board, the hero of "X the Unknown" was changed to another, somewhat generic scientist figure, played by American Dean Jagger. While we might despair that we lost out on a chance for many more Quatermass films on varying subjects by different writers, we can at the same time respect Kneale for his staunch effort to defend and protect the integrity of his creation from all comers, even those offering him large sums of money to "sell-out".

With the resulting film was made with Dean Jagger's scientist hero standing in for the good Professor, "X the Unknown" continued to prove that horror was a winner for Hammer and more Quatermass adaptations would evetually follow, the subsequent ones with Kneale's involvement.

Kneale would soon return to TV science fiction with an adaptation of George Orwell's "1984", itself a massive television landmark, which shocked and provoked viewers which its tale of Winston Smith's (Peter Cushing) struggle and crushing defeat at the hands of Big Brother.

This was followed by two more serials about his heroic Professor character, "Quatermass Two" and "Quatermass and the Pit". Hammer would subsequently make movies of both Q2 and the Pit.

Kneale would finally deliver a fourth serial at the end of the 1970s simply called "Quatermass", but also shown under the title "The Quatermass Conclusion."

This final serial would see the death of the Professor, giving his life heroically to defeat one last alien threat to the planet Earth and it people.

And we can only wonder if he chose to kill Quatermass to finally put an end to the ambition of others such as Hammer and the BBC to cash in and sell out Quatermass for the sake of sales and money.

However, Kneale was not done with his most famous creation and would touch upon him again in a 90s radio production called The Quatermass Memoirs, a mix of radio play and documentary about the historical context of the serials.

Finally, the third version of The Quatermass Experiment would appear in 2005.

Once again it would be performed live on the BBC, this time as an experiment to see if 21st-century television could recapture some of the energy and danger of live TV drama from the 1950s.

Also, this version was done as a single movie-length broadcast.

But our investigation must begin at the beginning of all this, with the first of the three different versions of The Quatermass Experiment. So what was it really like, in 1953, to sit and watch the live transmission of the first episode of the Quatermass Experiment on the BBC?

How was it received by the great British viewing public?

Well, if myth and legend and word-of-mouth are to be believed...it was nothing short of terrifying!

Establishing Contact...

Watching it today, one can only wonder what the actors and technicians must have felt in the minutes leading up to the beginning of the broadcast of that first episode on a Saturday night in 1953. Obviously actors had done many stage performances in front of a live audience before, but in this case there was no audience in front of the actors, just cameras and technicians.

For this ground-breaking production, voice-overs and music had to be fed in live as with a radio play. The actors had to remember their lines, the blocking, every movement, every gesture as in a theatre play and the cameras had to be moved and focused correctly to capture the action. Not one mishap could be permitted or the whole production could fall apart.

The first episode even included a few brief inserts which must have proven challenging at the time to achieve. Firstly, the serial opens with a title sequence and graphics with the name Quatermass seemingly written in the clouds. The font looks like the text was written by a human finger dipped in white paint and painted on a sheet of glass.

The effect is quite eerie.

There is a voice over after the titles, as the camera pans around the set, which tells us that "an experiment is an operation designed to discover some unknown truth. It is also a risk" and introduces the idea that three men have blasted off from Australia "one morning" in a rocket on a mission to reach outer space, something which was still science fiction at the time of the broadcast, Yuri Gagarin's first manned space flight still yet to happen in the real world.

This voice over is accompanied by images of high altitude shots of the Earth and then the drama in the studio begins.

The early parts of the episode all take place in the control room of British Rocket Group, which is a very good depiction of the type of Mission Control area which the real NASA would use years later when sending men to the Moon.

This early sequence is riveting and although we don't see a spaceship, the voices and performances convince us that Quatermass and his team are indeed monitoring the flight of a space ship which has gone missing after veering off course.

The writer Kneale quickly demonstrates his masterful grasp of the television medium when the Professor uses a chart on the wall to indicate to a politician named Blaker what kind of flight path his rocket was supposed to take around the Earth and where it has actually gone.

This visualises the situation without actually showing us the action. Similarly, the Professor also uses a model of his nuclear rocket to demonstrate the idea of capsule and stage separation.

These visual elements, especially the model of the nuclear rocket, do an excellent job of conveying a visual into the mind of the audience, a substitute for miniature affects, and in our imagination we see everything the writer wants us to see.

In fact, it seems like the type of thing real science experts did on TV reports in the 60s, using models and charts to indicate what astronauts were doing on the Apollo missions.

Soon we learn that the rocket has crashed back to Earth and the episode shifts locations.

Interestingly, despite how good it is, this lengthy control room segment of the story was the first thing cut when Hammer made their big screen version, with director and co-script writer Val Guest choosing to begin the story at the moment the rocket crashes back to Earth.

The surviving TV episodes contain little that is better than this opening in the control complex of BRG. Part of the reason it's so good is to do with the way it was done, not just the great scripting.

The situation is exciting and dramatic but it's the sense that all of this was being performed live and broadcast live as it was happening that creates the most tension.

In fact, it almost feels like you're watching this with a time-bomb ticking under your seat, just waiting to explode at any moment, the tension on screen is quite palpable at times and the intensity is reflected in the performances of the actors.

When the first episode changes scenes to the setting of a destroyed house where the spacecraft has crashed back to Earth, the drama and intensity finally lightens up somewhat and we are treated to some examples of humour and comedic characters, something which might seem unexpected, but which was quite intentional.

The actor who would later play Sam Seeley in the 1970 Doctor Who serial Spearhead from Space, a story designed to deliberately add a Quatermass-like flavour to Doctor Who's seventh season, turns up at the rocket crash site. He is a very stagy and comical as a London Bobby.

But first on the scene at the crash site is the character of Len and his hysterical wife. These two are also quite comical and there is a little old lady who is more preoccupied with looking after her cat Henry than anything else.

She is written as an intentionally comical character, pointing at the crashed rocket and asking "has that thing gone off yet?"

But it is the character of journalist James Fullalove which really makes the next big impression on the audience.

Paul Whitsun-Jones, later to portray the villainous Marshall in the Doctor Who serial "The Mutants", plays the reporter whose dialogue sparkles with wit and sarcasm. To give but one example, when a siren is heard in the distance, Fullalove remarks "Oh, they've sent an ambulance for me! How touching!"

It soon becomes apparent what we're watching here. This is not merely a space opera science fiction story, nor is it a horror story.

This is pop culture at its most inventive, part part science fiction, part horror story, part detective thriller and part light comedy. In fact, this serial is a mash up of genres and it has something for everyone.

It is truly a story aimed at the masses and its popular appeal is not surprising. Kneale is inventing the very template for popular television, in all its genre mixing, trope-combining glory.

Best of all, the first episode ends with a truly shocking cliffhanger ending. Viewers apparently shrieked and grasped and hid behind the sofa when the door to the space craft suddenly opened and something moved inside it.

The anticipation must have been feverish because at this point almost anything might have popped out, or leaped out, to terrorise the characters and the audience. In fact the script even has Fullalove describing it as, " the same elementary excitement children feel when they play pass the parcel."

So what does come out and how does this first episode end?

A space suited figure comes crashing out of the capsule and collapses. The Professor races into the opened ship and looks for the other two men, but realises to his horror that the other two men who were inside the spacecraft are gone.

They have disappeared, quite literally vanished into thin air, leaving just empty space suits.

As the Professor grabs the one surviving astronaut, Victor Carroon and shakes him, demanding to know what happened, the screen blacks out and the end credits roll.

More of exciting and dramatic music accompanies these credits and then a charming BBC announcer of the 1950s informs us that we will be able to see part two next Saturday night on the BBC.

One can only begin to imagine the impact this had on the British public at the time and how much episode two was anticipated eagerly by excited viewers across the country.

But along with the space age, the era of exciting TV science fiction had begun!

A Monstrous Concept...

The second episode of the Quatermass Experiment begins to develop the plot beyond the return of missing astronauts.

Professor Quatermass is now faced with the mystery of why only one astronaut has emerged from his rocket rather than the three he sent up.

This second episode involves many scenes in a dimly lit hospital room, featuring the astronaut Victor (Duncan Lamont, who would return to Quatermass as drill operator Sladden for the Hammer film of Quatermass and the Pit and inevitably appear in Doctor Who as an irate Scotsman in "Death to the Daleks") and various scenes of Fullalove and Scotland Yard's Inspector Lomax pondering the mystery along with the Professor.

The concept of the alien menace which emerges over the course of the serial is actually far more sophisticated and interesting than most people seem to remember or believe.

The generally held notion is that the Quatermass Experiment is about a man who begins to mutate into a monster and in the most simplistic terms this would appear to be true.

However the concept as presented in the script is far more sophisticated than a simple case of a man changing into an alien creature.

In actual fact, an alien life-form which takes the form of pure energy, a kind of living cosmic ray, has passed through the space capsule while it was lost out in deep space and, one by one, this life force has absorbed each of the three men.

It has formed one, single body for itself to live inside, as a means of adapting to our environment, but the misleading factor is that the creature looks like the last thing it assimilated!

Since Victor Carroon was the third astronaut to be assimilated, the creature looks like Victor, but inside this body which looks like Victor at face value, is the suppressed, traumatised and confused minds and memories of all three astronauts! As Kneale put it, the creature is three men melded into one!

This concept leads to a fascinating and genuinely unnerving sequence in the second episode when Victor is confronted with the wife of one of the other astronauts, Louisa Green, wife of astronaut Charles Green. (Peter Bathurst, later to appear in Doctor Who's "Claws of Axos" as the buffoon Chinn, as well as an appearance in Barry Letts and Terrance Dicks' "Moonbase 3").

Although it appears she is talking to Victor, she reacts as if she is talking to her husband what appears to be Victor calls the other astronauts wife by the nickname he always used for her, "Lou", short for Louisa.

This is then put to the test by the Professor. The script establishes clearly that one of the other astronauts, Reichenheim, spoke German and was German.

However, Victor did not speak any German at all. When questioned in German, the man, or creature, who appears to be Victor, is able to answer in complete sentences and correct technical details, in German!

In this ingenious way, the script conveys the horrifying idea that the minds or spirits of the missing men are somehow inside what appears to be Victor, the seemingly lone survivor.

In this way, we have a kind of Demonic possession story, but the concept is much more interesting than just another case of a man possessed by the devil.

The script actually gives us a metaphor for the Cold War fear of Communism, loss of identity, individuals being absorbed into the unity which robs them of their individuality, their personality and their freedom.

And even today, long after the Cold War, the metaphor still retains power and resonance, as well as relevance, because it relates to many other ways in which our individuality is challenged, even threatened, by systems and forms of control.

The four episodes which were not retained on film dramatise the hospitalised Victor being abducted, only to kill one of his kidnappers and go on the run in England. Soon, a police search begins for the missing "man" and finally the thing which appears to be Victor changes, as he comes into contact with plant life and animal life, absorbing them and taking on the appearance of a mass of plant life.

Some of his victims include a cactus and some swans. The image of this man, covered in plant life, is apparently intended by Kneale to resemble the mythical image of the so-called Green Man. Kneale's ability to incorporate mythology into his storytelling is one of his most striking trade marks and would appear again in the notable example of Quatermass and the Pit.

By the end of the serial the alien creature has become a gigantic, tendril-dangling mass of plant life which is located inside Poet's Corner, Westminster Abbey.

The script ingeniously has the creature discovered during a live TV broadcast and the writer Kneale himself devised the simple but ingenious visual effects which bring the monster to convincing and terrifying life. (This was due to the BBC's attitude of "you wrote it, you do it", according to Kneale).

One only needs to look at the surviving photographic still of the creature to realise why it was considered so convincing at the time and why it is remembered as the monster which shocked and terrified the nation.

Created by attaching bits and pieces of real plants, real roots and bark to a pair of latex-covered leather gardening gloves, the monster is remarkably convincing and realistic.

In fact, far more realistic than most subsequent attempts at similar creatures created by dedicated miniature effects teams, such as the one seen in the Hammer movie and the Krynoid monster from the Quatermass Experiment homage in Doctor Who's "Seeds of Doom".

Apparently, Kneale wore the gloves himself with his hands dangling through a hole which had been cut out of a black-and-white photographic blow-up of the interior of Westminster Abbey.

When this was shown on the TV monitor, Kneale simply twitched his hands in small, subtle ways to give the creature a sense of life and movement. This provided a truly chilling cliffhanger ending to the fifth episode of the TV serial.

In the finale of the final episode of the TV serial, the Professor courageously confronts the monster inside the Abbey and speaks to the three minds of the missing astronauts who lay dormant inside the creature's mass.

This is presaged by a realisation that the plant-like mass is about to release spores which could cause all life on Earth to be assimilated, in effect a threat to destroy the world as we know it.

And in this dramatic scene, in Poet's Corner, he appeals to them to resist, to use their willpower and to break free from this alien force which has consumed them. "You must dissever from it!" he tells them, "You three...as men...must die!"

And as they finally break free, the minds of the three missing astronauts actually destroy the body of the alien creature, tearing it apart, proving the human spirit is far more powerful than this alien force which consumed their physical bodies.

Quatermass discovers one of the dangling tendrils is now dry and stiff as particles of the plant-like creature fall, like Autumn leaves, all around him.

This ending is a kind of exorcism scene and Quatermass establishes himself as a modern day Dr Van Helsing, a monster hunter for the space age.

But since he is also guilty of bringing this monstrous threat to Earth, he can also be seen as a contemporary Dr. Frankenstein, to an extent, the creator of the terrifying menace which he must confront and defeat.

With its mix of Gothic horror, science fiction and detective-style storytelling, as well as humorous asides, mythology and topicality of themes, the Quatermass Experiment is virtually where the writer Kneale invents and creates popular television entertainment as we know it today.

The influence of the serial was seen many times in the decades which followed, too, in notable TV series such as Pathfinders in Space, Doctor Who, the Gerry and Sylvia Anderson series UFO and later in the American series the X-Files.

The Actors.

Reginald Tate.

Now let's talk about the people behind the show...

In the first live performance of the serial/story on the BBC, the part of the Professor was played by Reginald Tate, an actor who the writer Nigel Kneale described as having "a great attack" in the role. Presumably this means he approached the script and the performance with energy, enthusiasm and focus.

On screen, Tate is superb as the dedicated and determined Professor. He is intelligent, thoughtful, sensitive and determined to save his astronauts, determined to find answers and explanations and then, finally, to save the world itself.

The character as he plays it also has a tendency to flare up in sudden anger but then pull it back, restrain himself and go forward in a calmer, more thoughtful and controlled manner.

Kneale was apparently very happy with Tate in the role and saw much more for him. But, sadly, things did not go according to plan. Tate could have become a huge legend of popular culture for his acting as the Professor, much in the same way that William Hartnell did as the first Doctor Who. By all accounts, the writer and producer both wanted him to continue on playing the Professor Quatermass role in subsequent serials and if this had happened, he may have become known as the only actor associated with the role.

Also, there was even talk that he might have played the role in the movie versions, had he been around when they were made.

Reginald Tate was also very keen on the fact that the serial had been a huge success but was disappointed by the fact that episodes 3,4,5 and 6 were not recorded. He apparently enrolled in the BBC director's course, intending to direct a second version of the The Quatermass Experiment himself. Had all gone as intended, a complete version of Quatermass Experiment could have existed today.

But, unfortunately, he never got to put the Quatermass Experiment on again and died suddenly and unexpectedly of a heart attack, just a matter of weeks before he was due to star in the second Quatermass serial.

As a result we are left with only two episodes as examples of his fine work in the role of the Professor.

Brian Donlevy.

For Hammer's movie version of the serial, retitled Quatermass Xperiment (a play on the film's X rating), American actor Brian Donlevy was brought in to play the Professor. It was standard practice to hire an American actor to help British films gain American distribution deals at the time. Donlevy had a reputation for playing tough guys with a heart and was something of veteran actor in Hollywood.

Donlevy was much more heavily built than Reginald Tate and brought a steam-rolling, relentless and perhaps slightly callous quality to the role. Writer Nigel Kneale spoke many times over the years about how unhappy he was to see his intellectual Quatermass portrayed as a tough, aggressive American.

However, the director Val Guest felt that Donlevy was down to Earth and made the way-out story line seem believable. Many critics agree that Brian Donlevy's performance is down to Earth, believable and compelling and that he gives the movie version of the Professor an intensity and authority which helps make the film a very compelling viewing experience.

Donlevy would return to the role for the sequel, Quatermass 2, making him one of the only actors to portray the character more than once. His performance in the second film is notably more refined and sees Donlevy much surer of who exactly his character is. One criticism levelled at Donlevy was that he had a drinking problem and that he was visibly intoxicated in the films. However, director Guest disputed this claim, saying Donlevy certainly was a drinker, but was never drunk on set to an extent that affected his work.

Jason Flemyng.

For the 2005 live TV broadcast of The Quatermass Experiment, produced as part of a concept called TV on Trial, actor Jason Fleming played the role of Professor Quatermass as a much younger man than we had ever seen before.

This updated version of the Professor was a step away from the rocketry pioneer of the 50s. Instead, the 2005 Quatermass Experiment redefines the character as an independent scientist analogous to billionaire Richard Branson, of Virgin. Like Branson, this Quatermass is involved in a privately funded enterprise to send men into space.

Although low key and understated in the part, Jason Flemyng is believable and effective as the thoughtful but deeply troubled Professor. Unlike the original live version, this Quatermass Experiment went out as a single movie length live broadcast and the actors were committed to a marathon performance. Flemyng is very dependable from start to end. Like Tate and Donlevy before him, he inhabits the role with the respect and presence it deserves.

But whichever version you prefer, most viewers will agree that all the actors who have played Professor Quatermass have brought talent, authority and intelligence to the role.

Context and Legacy

To put Quatermass into its historical context, we must consider the beginning and the end of the space age, the so-called Space Race, the political propaganda and fears about Russia and Communism that went with it, the chilly sense of uncertainty and the brooding threat of a possible nuclear war, and much more besides.

The first serial as broadcast on the BBC has already been described as ground-breaking and there's no doubt that for Hammer horror films, the movie version of the story, Quatermass Xperiment, was also a remarkable and influential achievement.

The third Quatermass Experiment, however, represented something quite different because by 2005, Britain's place in modern popular culture had become overshadowed by an increasing tendency towards domination from the United States from Hollywood.

British television science fiction was making a comeback in 2005 with the rebirth of Doctor Who, under Russell T Davies, starring Christopher Eccleston. At the time, Doctor Who was aiming to be loud and colourful, vibrant and full of cutting-edge CGI special effects.

Because of this context, the style of the 2005 Quatermass Experiment then seemed almost old-fashioned, low key and low tech, taking a storyline originally broadcast in the 50s and doing a live broadcast again.

However, 10 years on also we can see, with some objectivity, that the 2005 version of Quatermass is both well scripted and well acted and has a sombre, eerie mood and atmosphere, thanks to its combination of X-Files-inspired lighting and documentary style imagery of news reports, industrial settings and ominous aerial shots of the city of London in the evening, its red-lit streets looking for all the world like the arteries and blood stream of a giant living body, now infected by the thing which came back to Earth in the BRG rocket ship and broke free.

Even in the 21st century, Quatermass continues to work as storytelling, continues to impress with its ideas and central character, continues to possess potential for more. Perhaps another Quatermass story might emerge in the future to thrill and chill us all over again...

A Fearful Influence

The legacy of the Quatermass Experiment lies in its long lasting popularity and its wide reaching influence on other TV shows and movies .

Film director John Carpenter for example has spoken about how seminal and original the Hammer movie version of the Quatermass Experiment seemed when he saw the trailer for it in the United States.

The Doctor Who TV series was famously influenced by all of the Quatermass serials on many occasions, but some notable examples have included The Seeds of Doom and Meglos, which drew on the idea of the cactus on a human face and hands.

Seeds of Doom itself appears to have been influenced by the Avengers' episode The Man Eater of Surrey Green, which was a rather brief, small scale version of the plot line of Quatermass Experiment.

The first instance of people becoming infected and mutating into monsters on Doctor Who was in Jon Pertwee's season seven, the year the Doctor Who first began to seriously emulate Nigel Kneales Professor .

In the story Inferno, people become infected by a green slime coming from deep underground at the Inferno drilling project and this slime causes anyone who comes into contact with it to transform into green-skinned, snarling monsters referred to in the script and end credits as Primords, a reference to the primordial slime.

The character of Noah, in the early Tom Baker serial the Ark in Space, undergoes a Carroon style transformation into a monster, while Peter Davison chases a decaying man with green lumps on his face and hands through city streets in Arc on Infinity.

There is also a high level of influence in the Gerry and Sylvia Anderson TV series UFO. Many episodes of UFO depict people becoming possessed or controlled by aliens. In one episode called The Man Who Came Back, the plot is very reminiscent of the Quatermass Experiment as it begins with an astronaut going missing during his return to the Earth from space and when he's found, it slowly becomes apparent that he is different, zombie-like.

The ending of the episode however is similar to the finale of the TV version of Quatermass 2. Other UFO episodes such as Kill Straker, Long Sleep and ESP have some aspects which seem reminiscent of the Kneale's serial.

The later Anderson series Space:1999 would also return to Kneale influenced plots with Force of Life, about a man who is possessed by an alien force which feeds of heat and energy.

The influence of Nigel Kneale's opus finally reached the United States in a major way in 1993 with the beginning of the TV series the X-Files.

Created by Chris Carter, the series contained a story arc about aliens coming to Earth and a government conspiracy of silence to cover it up, frustrating the investigations of Mulder and Scully.

This series would go on to draw upon all of Nigel Kneale's work in much the same way that Doctor Who had before but perhaps making it less obvious and even seeming at times like its writers felt they were saying something new, instead of doing a homage.

This had the effect of leaving some disgruntled fans to eventually accuse Chris Carter of stealing his myth arc from Kneale, particularly with the movie Fight the Future which seemed like a 90s remake of Q2.

Changes.

Perhaps the most controversial change in the Hammer movie Quatermass Xperiment is that the entire ending in which the Professor confronts the creature and talks to the suppressed minds of his three astronaut friends is missing.

Instead, the monster is dispatched almost as soon as it is discovered and it is destroyed in a very matter-of-fact way, more suited to American horror movies of the day. The creature is simply barbecued by giving it a massive jolt of electricity.

However the film ends on a remarkable note as Professor Quatermass turns his back on the tragic deaths of his friends and the near catastrophe which has just been averted and walks away, stating he wants to start again.

We see the Professor walk away with a determination which is nothing short of breath-taking and moments later the film ends as another rocket roars into the sky, no doubt heading straight back out into space where Carroon and his two fellow astronauts have just come from.

This is the final note almost manages to compensate for the loss of Kneale's original ending as it hammer s home the idea that the human spirit is not just determined to go out and explore space but that it is bloody-minded to the point of obsession and won't let anything stop it, not even the threat of catastrophe or the deaths of innocent people! Undeniably, it is a remarkable ending .

The 2005 Quatermass Experiment reinstates both the early Mission control style scenes at the British Rocket Group as well as giving us a chance to finally see Kneale's original ending, as Quatermass talks to the minds of the three astronauts.

Perhaps the biggest disappointment here is that the monster itself is never seen, only implied or suggested.

However, a surreal moment in which the three missing astronauts appear out of the darkness manages to make up for the lack of a visible monster.

It might have been nice to see how the creature could have been rendered with modern day CGI special effects but nevertheless simply iplying and suggesting a monster through dialogue is perhaps more suitable considering the whole live performance has a low budget, documentary style realism to its feel and CG FX might have jarred with this kind of atmosphere.

Some of the dialogue in the 2005 broadcast is obscured by background noise, too, however if one listens carefully and then it is quite potent when the weary and yet relieved Professor emerges at the end from the Tate Modern and announces to his friends, and the worried crowd, that Reichenheim, Green and Corroon have won their battle!

Overall the 2005 version is a success and proved to be one of the most popular programs ever broadcast on BBC Four.

Once again Kneale's opus proved to be a winner. All three versions of the story are well worth seeing and the published book of the script by Nigel Kneale is also exceptionally well written and makes for an absolutely gripping and compelling reading experience.

Perhaps the best way to fully appreciate just what Nigel Kneale wrote is to read the script and view all three versions.

Although there are only the first two episodes of the original six part story, those two episodes constitute more than an hour of viewing time and serve as a solid introduction to the story.

The movie version certainly captures the main body of the story very effectively and shows us the monster and the live 2005 version brings it into colour and into a more modern age and gives us an opportunity to see a dramatisation of the original ending where human minds and human spirits struggle to break free from the alien force which has consumed them.

By watching all three and reading the script book, one is left with the conclusion that the Quatermass Experiment is a remarkable piece of work and it stands as a testimony to the fact that the writer Nigel Kneale ,who had a strong sense of story and theme and believed in the power and value of words, could leave an enormous impact and a lasting legacy, despite whatever technical limitations or unhappy twists of fate may have attempted to get in his way.

Like the good Professor himself, Nigel Kneale was determined, intelligent and quite an unstoppable force!

Quatermass Two

And its

Legacy

Episode one:

The Bolts.

A British military exercise is underway and soldiers are being trained in the use of radar equipment mounted on the roofs of trucks in the middle of the wilderness. Suddenly the radar equipment picks up something coming down from space.

At first, the object appears to be be a meteorite and on a nearby farming property, an old farmer on a tractor reacts to a roaring sound as something speeds overhead and strikes the Earth. Moments later, he goes to investigate and finds a steaming meteorite crater.

Upon leaving the radar testing area, Captain John Dillon and another soldier drive away and as they drive they discuss recent UFO sightings and other reports of things falling from the sky and the fact that it has all been covered up with strict orders from the army to never mention UFOs again.

Suddenly they come upon a distraught woman. She is the wife of the farmer and she leads Dillon and the other soldier to the farmer who now crouches in the field in a strange state of mind.

Dillon examines fragments of the meteorite and decides to take them to see his father-in-law to be, Professor Quatermass, the so-called rocket-man at the British rocket group.

The Professor is dressed in protective coveralls at present and using an instrument like a Geiger counter to conduct an examination of the nuclear motor of the Quatermass two rocket, one of a pair of twin rockets built to his new design.

He is informed that his examination was practically a post-mortem, by friend and colleague Dr Pugh. The Professor is in a bitter mood and we soon find out why when his daughter Paula plays a film report put together by an Australian man named Webster who also narrates the film.

The film shows a team of rocketry personnel preparing to launch the other of the twin rockets, the second nuclear powered rocket from the Professor's designs, in the desert in Northern Australia. Everything goes wrong and the rocket explodes, with the force of a thermonuclear bomb, and everyone on the rocket project is annihilated. The Professor hangs his head in despair, he uncovers a painting of a base on the moon, announcing that his moon project is over and in fact, his career seems over because the disaster in Australia has all but destroyed his reputation. Now the use of nuclear engines is frowned upon as far too dangerous ever to use again.

Suddenly Dillon arrives and snaps the Professor out of his mood by showing him the meteorite fragments. Quatermass's assistant Dr Leo Pugh examines the fragments and realises that the meteorite was a hollow shell, probably with something inside it.

Quatermass goes with Dillon to investigate. First, the pair go to see the Plowman from the farm and his wife but when they get there they find that he has undergone a change of personality and he is now sullen, grumpy, angry and antisocial and he insists that they leave. The Professor has no choice but to walk away and leave the woman with this dangerously changed man.

At the pub nearby, the Professor and Dillon learn from an old man about the destruction of the town of Winnerden Flats for the building of a research complex.

As they search the destroyed remains of the small village, the Professor is astonished to see a refinery or plant which bears and uncanny resemblance in shape to his proposed moon project, a means of colonising another world, but the question is obvious: just what is such a complex doing on Earth in the middle of England?

Suddenly meteorites fall and as they rush to investigate, the Professor and Dillon get a nasty shock. One meteorite seems to burst, ejecting gas, and Dillon collapses, the Professor exclaiming in horror, " Dillon... there's something on your face!"

Behind the Scenes

If you ever doubted Nigel Kneale's reputation as a master craftsman of the television medium, the script for Q2 demonstrates his skill in spades. Drawing techniques from theatre, film and radio drama, Kneale conveys his plot details with both pace and punch , despite the fact that this was still the days of live TV.

The opening features location film of radar trucks and a jeep arriving. This was a pre-filmed insert added in live after the titles sequence by telecine, a once common technique of aiming a video camera at a movie screen onto which film is projected.

The timing is all important as the film must roll in time for the camera to broadcast its images. The vision switches to the live studio where actors perform the radar training scene.

The scene ends with lingering close ups of the instrument panel and eerie music, a good way to allow for a smooth transition to another film insert showing Dillon driving away. This switches to Dillon and fellow soldier seated in the truck in studio.

A studio hand moves something long and thin past a light to create a shadow sweeping over the actors while the illusion is almost ruined by the shadow of a crouching technician crossing the white backdrop behind the supposedly driving truck.

Another switch to film is used when Dillon meets the ploughman and his wife. We switch to a model shot of the Q2 rocket.

Clifford Hatts built a set for the base of the rocket which is a reasonable match for the base of the model and the vision mixer switches to this set where John Robinson appears at last, clad in a plastic Mac and waving a fairly convincing prop around.

Robinson had been cast at the eleventh hour following the sudden death of Reginald Tate, who had been slated to reprise his role from Quatermass Experiment, only to be struck down by a sudden and fatal heart attack.

While the protective suit is obviously not a true anti radiation suit, the scene allows Robinson to make a distinctive first impression.

Cutting away allows him time to change into his normal outfit, the hair people no doubt quickly brushing his hair into place before his next scene. We get some brilliant moments next.

Paula Quatermass, his daughter, aims a projector toward the camera and turns it on. We cut to a filmed insert which is supposedly what the projector is showing. The insert is a cleverly edited mix of real footage of a rocket base crew at work, model shots of a Quatermass rocket and footage of a real atomic explosion.

A voice over explains this as film of how the rocket test went wrong, killing everyone involved. Robinson seems to be under rehearsed here, possibly glancing for lines written on clip boards and elsewhere, but under tough circumstances manages to be a convincing and sympathetic Quatermass.

A painting of an artist's impression of the Moon Project is another clever device for visualising an idea as Quatermass describes it.

The possessed ploughman scene is impressive and troubling and while the actors at the pub struggle a little, Kneale impresses in the dialog.

The conspiracy theory plot with the government as the enemy, in bed with aliens, covering the truth and becoming an enemy to the people, seems a very modern idea, yet here it is, in part one, fully developed.

It's possible that Kneale drew influence from Orwell in this area.

It's never been stated on the record but Kneale scripted the BBC's 1984 and the idea of government as enemy is here with the old man saying "things was better when there was less government about. They spoil and destroy!"

The model of the alien plant, the government project, is impressive too. The story only falters at the cliffhanger when a meteorite bursts and the Professor cries "Dillon! There's something on your face."

The camera angle and reaction just doesn't quite work.

However the over all impact was more than enough to grab the audience.

The use of Mars as theme music and an impressive title scene using dry ice mist through the name Quatermass 2 give the impression of this as the same series continuing from Quatermass Experiment.

Review

The Bolts brings back Quatermass in fine style. The music of Holt's Mars packs a punch from the get go, resoundingly informing us that the show which terrified the nation in 1953 is back, bigger and bolder than ever.

From a modern perspective it might seem stately and filled with static camera shots but compared to the previous serial this is a step up in many ways.

The first serial changed settings and locations when needed but this episode has proper location filming with the cast, skilful switches to studio video, clever use of models and stock footage and it all moves at a good pace, picking up momentum in the last half.

John Robinson makes a tougher, more heroic Quatermass, now a man who puts on a trench coat and digs into an investigation in the style of a detective.

This is really the template for Dr Who and other British SF heroes to come.

Dr Leo Pugh is well played by Oscar winner Hugh Griffith of Ben Hur fame. Dillon and Paula are good too. But the star is the script and Rudi Cartier's amazing atmosphere of menace and fear.

Even when the roar of a meteorite is produced by a technician scraping his thumb nail over the mesh of a microphone, the sense of menace from space is palpable. It should be noted that the thumb nail scrape produces a reasonably good sound effect, too.

Episode Two

The Mark.

The story picks up from where it left off, this time with a much more convincing rendition of the Professor's reaction to Dillon collapsing after being stung by whatever shot out of the bursting hollow meteorite.

As the professor tries to help his future son-in-law, a truck arrives, whistles sound and the professor is face-to-face with the zombies, helmeted guards carrying machine guns, their faces marked with scar tissue. The scars are the mark.

At first it is not made clear what's going on but the mark of alien possession is analogous to the mark of the beast in Christianity, a sign of Satanic possession.

Dillon's personality changes and as the zombies try to take him away in their truck, he turns against the Professor, warming him not to follow. The Professor is forced away at gunpoint and made to leave, but instead he picks his way through the ruins of the destroyed town looking for answers, staring at the ominous plant with its huge pressure domes.

Suddenly he's confronted by a tramp who recounts the story of the destruction of the town and the building of the complex. Quatermass heads to a nearby village, a prefabricated town, to look for help, but when he gets there he finds posters on the wall telling people to keep their lips sealed and not talk about their work.

His attempts to get help are turned down by the unhelpful members of the town committee. He also encounters a mother and child and realises the child is possessed after finding one of the meteorites.

As he is given the cold shoulder, he is again forced to walk away, leaving the unwary mother with her alien possessed daughter, who is staring into space with cold, glassy eyes back.

Back in London the professor goes to the Ministry and demands answers about the plant.

He discovers that it is supposedly a government project for the manufacture of synthetic food.

With the help of strong-willed politician called Broadhead, who has been trying to force an inquiry into the activities of the plant, the professor is able to get into a top-level government meeting where a number of powerful, important government men take their seats around a table.

Suddenly, Quatermass is shocked to see that one of them has the horrific scar-like mark of alien possession on his face.

It seems the British public have been right all along about their government, if this cliffhanger is anything to go by, public servants really are inhuman monsters...

Behind the Scenes

Episode two is a more successful production over all, than The Bolts. Kneale's script requires less visual effects this time and less goes wrong. The scenes continue to switch from filmed inserts and live studio performances on the fine sets built at the BBC.

Robinson is better rehearsed and has less technical dialog, turning in a more polished performance. The location shoot includes getting footage of the view through the windshield of the Professor's car as it drives to the town.

The simple use of posters on a wall manages to convey the secrecy and the cast use theatre technique to sign post to the audience when someone is possessed, the camera moving in close on the staring eyes of the little girl.

Fowler at the Ministry unveils evidence about the food plant with files and photographs to suggest his evidence.

The scar which represents the mark is not very clear and the zombie guards at the alien plant are not very well acted. Perhaps the most striking aspect is the opening montage of clips from part one with a narration recapping, a device not possible on Quatermass Experiment.

Over all the production team accomplishes a more polished piece of television than before.

Broadhead represents another good guest cast appearance as does the tramp. Wilfred Bramble as the Tramp is polished and professional, despite the rough character he plays, displaying the skill that would later make him a star in Steptoe and Son. Rupert Davies as Vincent Broadhead is equally strong and would go on to be famous for playing Maigret, among other things.

Notably it seems the tramp is recapping the backstory of Winnerden Flats, possibly because the old man in episode one struggled with line delivery. Kneale may have been asked to write this as an 11th hour add on.

Whatever the case, Cartier's direction goes smoothly and the results are strong by the standards of the period.

Review

The Mark is not as science fiction heavy as The Bolts, dealing instead with humans being obstructive. There are no real effects this time around but a focus on actors and dialog alone.

There some good pre-filmed location work early on but it all ends up in the world of politics and committees.

Maybe a less fun episode, but the sense of a conspiracy of silence and a singular lack of cooperation gives the whole thing an uneasy feeling. It's a generally more polished episode and shows the serial and BBC drama as a whole going from strength to strength.

With nary a slip anywhere, this is a solid piece of television.

The zombified little girl and the reveal of the mark on the face of a committee meeting mean there's enough implication here to chill the audience and it kept them coming back for more, as one might expect.

Episode Three:

The Food.

After seeing the mark on members of the meeting, the Professor sticks his neck out by producing Dr Pugh's plaster reconstruction of one of the hollow meteorites which has a distinctive shape, showing it to the committee.

They react with shock and almost a hungry stare. But one of them becomes angry and Quatermass has to leave. Pugh and Paula form a theory that the meteorites could be coming from an asteroid permanently hidden in the shadow of the Earth and invisible to astronomers.

With the aid of a man called Ward, the Prof and Fowler get inside the plant at Winnerden flats.

Meanwhile the zombies kill a whole family who are picnicking nearby. Suddenly the Prof realises Ward is missing.

And then he appears, staggering down from a giant tank, his whole body covered in black food slime.

He collapses at Quatermass's feet and dies instantly. The Professor and Fowler narrowly escape the plant with a sample of the slime.

At the rocket base Dr Pugh detects the asteroid on its way towards Earth!

Behind the Scenes:

Another very efficient production with effects men Jack Kine and Bernard Wilkie introducing a very Dr Who-style model of a giant radio telescope dish at the rocket group which is used as an establishing shot for the scenes of Quatermass, Fowler, Pugh and Paula at the end. The BBC managed to get radar equipment loaned to the production by Her Majesty's War Office and this made its debut in The Bolts.

Here we see more electronic gear, possibly related stuff, as Pugh tracks the alien asteroid. Rudolf Cartier uses lights below Dr Pugh in the finale to give his face an eerie under-lighting effect, possibly suggesting his face is lit by the glow of the instruments.

The episode also features a very lengthy sequence of location work filmed at the Shell Haven plant in Essex. This same plant would be reused by director Val Guest for Hammer Film's remake of the serial a couple of years later, as would, apparently, the helmets and other gear worn by the zombie guards.

Perhaps the most remarkable accomplishment of the episode is the covering of the actor playing Ward in a glistening oil-like layer of liquid to simulate the synthetic (and poisonous) food which covers him. He appears this way both on location at Shell Haven and in the cut to studio where he collapses.

There is no record of how the actor felt about being covered in black slime or what it was made from, but it's well documented that the actor who suffered the same fate in the Hammer film version made a number of jokes about how he was an important man in acting circles, yet this was how he was treated!

Review

The Food is a much more potent episode than what we have seen so far. The tour of the Shell Have Refinery is lengthy but well worth it, giving the episode an impressive cinematic sense of scale.

While the plant does not closely resemble the model plant seen in The Bolts, it is easy to accept that we are seeing part of the complex from ground level. The sight of armed guards and a distinctive use of signs gives the idea this is not Shell Refinery, but something more sinister.

The girl who waitresses and serves coffee in the Espresso bar is delightfully hammy and over played, but Ward is a much better character and his death is one of the most shocking moments in the history of television.

Staggering down the steps, covered in black muck, eyes closed and mouth open in grotesque agony, his hand smears the slime all over the side of the giant tank before he falls at Quatermass ' feet, as dead as a coffin nail.

It's brutal, grisly horror which packs a punch.

Even better still, Kneale brings this potential cliffhanger forward in the narrative, landing this blow early so we have time to let it sink in before he lets the episode wrap up on a second, less shocking but suitably effective cliffhanger, giving the serial a feeling of ending the episode on a double-whammy.

It's small wonder then that the following episode opened with a stern warning from the BBC that the show was not suitable for children... or those of you who may have a nervous disposition!

Episode four:

The Coming.

The Professor discusses the nature of the alien menace with Fowler and Paula now, theorising and speculating, and he describes the alien menace as a living thing which was encased in the hollow meteorite shell, living on gases such as ammonia gas and methane gas.

He says he believes that it was only able to survive a few moments in Earth 's atmosphere and when released, it died expending itself upon the nearest human target, such as John Dillon. He is notably insensitive to his daughter's feelings at this point.

He goes on to say that death may not matter to the alien life force because when it dies it invades the human nervous system, delivering a kind of mental sting and is able to take over the will of the subject.

He says he believes he saw it clinging to Dillon's face like a dark bubble just for a few moments before it burst, no doubt leaving a mark as it entered. He goes on to say that he believes the aliens to be part of a colonial organism and that what is known to one would be known by all, experience itself would be shared and communicated.

His friends ask more questions and he tells them he thinks these things are coming from one of the outer planets perhaps a moon of one of the outer planets, where the atmosphere is methane and ammonia, a frozen world.

Paula also puts forward the idea that the asteroid which is sending the meteorites is artificially made, not a natural asteroid, with its own internal atmosphere and support system. It seems it has been driven towards the Earth for the purpose of sending down the hollow meteorite shells, which are the product of mathematics and exact engineering.

Next Quatermass calls upon a journalist named Conrad and asks him for an urgent meeting to discuss the flying objects scare and Winnerden Flats.

Conrad is surprised to discover that most of the documentation in his newspapers files about old UFO sightings seems to be gone missing, almost as if there is a conspiracy to remove information about UFOs and things falling from the sky from his archives!

When he meets up with the Professor, he is sceptical at first but later goes with him to the prefab town of the workers who helped build the pressure domes of the giant alien plant.

At a pub the Professor and Conrad meet the locals, but when the locals realise that Conrad is trying to pump them for information which is regarded as secret, they turn hostile.

But one of the so called over-shots, a meteorite shell, lands at that moment, hitting the pub.

Quatermass and Conrad go to investigate as many more meteorites come whistling down out of the sky. Realising that this is the coming of the aliens, the beginning of the invasion, Quatermass becomes determined to get inside one of the pressure domes.

He disguises himself as one of the zombie guards and puts on a gas mask to get inside.

Meanwhile Conrad returns to the pub and calls his newspaper, trying to alert them to the alien menace. He also reveals that he has been exposed one of the meteorites! As he struggles against his mind being taken over by the alien control, Conrad tries to tell the story which astonishes and horrifies workers nearby who overhear him.

Meanwhile, inside the plant, the Professor opens an inspection window and looks inside inside one of the pressure domes.

He sees the horrifying sight of the huge, slimy, alien Amonid creatures, which are growing, thriving, undulating, rising up out of the black food slime, swelling in size, combining and changing shape, as if to form some kind of horrific monster… a terrifying threat to all Mankind!

Behind the Scenes

Once again, Cartier continues to shoot his actors in studio as they perform their live dialog and interactions like a play, but with plenty of filmed inserts to liven things up.

The location filming at Shell Haven plant in Essex seems to have gone smoothly although there were claims that wind-up cameras had to be used on the subsequent movie version due to concerns that electrical equipment might cause a fire.

The zombie guard uniforms which appear in the TV series are supposedly reused in the Hammer film, according to Val Guest.

Roger Delgado is given lengthy monologues and delivers them effectively, never appearing to suffer any trouble remembering all the words, no doubt to the relief of the director.

Some filmed inserts, on the other hand, seem to have not played in time for the vision mixer to cut them into the action, and so John Robinson has to point out men and trucks over there and over this way, etc, to cover for the issue.

Various liquids and gunge are used for the tank FX shot. Pieces of rubber and plastic were used to amazing effect to simulate the rising of the Amonid monsters out of the food slime by Jack Kine and Bernard Wilkie.

Review:

Kneale's ideas are amazing, his plotting is top notch and he knows all the horror elements to put in for shocks and scares, but the thing that makes his work so good, is the dialog. Kneale's dialog is so good, so engaging and so rich with food for thought, that you are carried along, even if the picture quality is relatively poor by today's HD standards.

If I had to single out one thing that makes Kneale the best, it's his dialog. To give but one of many, many examples. Fowler: "But you said the thing inside dies." Quatermass: "That may not matter." Fowler: "Death not matter?" And when he explains that it enters the brain and overwhelms the whole system, Fowler says: "A sort of... mental sting?"

Just look at that choice of words. A mental sting, like a bee or a hornet, stinging the brain. Imagery like that in dialog just doesn't come along very often.

And Delgado ahoy! Yes, The Coming is most noteworthy as the episode which features an early appearance in BBC science fiction from Roger Delgado.

Delgado was a brilliant actor, a man who understood how powerful men behave, and his suave presence graced a large number of Doctor Who episodes in the Jon Pertwee era of the 1970s as The Master, a ruthless yet charming rival Time Lord who became a thorn in the good Doctor's side.

Delgado was so popular as the villainous Master than Pertwee felt his own popularity would be overshadowed.

Tragically, Delgado was killed at the peak of his Doctor Who success when his taxi crashed, shortly after he flew to an overseas location to shoot a new film role.

Despite his passing, Delgado left behind a long lasting legacy that saw the Master returned many times played by other actors.

But Dr Who fans often maintain no one was as good as the original. Delgado lacks his trademark beard in

The Coming but his acting chops are on full display as Conrad, a very good ally for the troubled Quatermass and his final scene, succumbing to the alien control which has invaded him, is a shining moment where we see just what a great talent the world lost when Delgado's life was cut short.

The Coming is also famous for the opening being preceded by the dire warning from the BBC, over an iconic emblam, stating "Before we begin tonight's episode of Quatermass 2, we should like to point out that in our opinion, it is not suitable for children… or those who may have a nervous disposition! "

Such an alarmed and unnerved response from the BBC's powers that be could only be taken as confirmation that Quatermass 2 was delivering on its promise to be as scary, if not more so, than the original Quatermass Experiment.

Episode five:

The Frenzy.

The workers who helped build the plant are so shocked and horrified at the fate of the journalist Hugh Conrad that they storm into the plant, armed with sticks and other hand held missiles, shouting and raging at authority, to demand answers.

This is much like a night time worker 's strike. As the workers riot and march up to the gates of the plant, the force their way inside, Quatermass finds that he is caught in the middle of it all.

When he is found looking in the inspection window at the undulating creatures, growing, changing form and size, the Amonid things from space, he is lucky to escape capture by the guards.

Soon the workers seize control of the pressure control room for the first completed pressure dome and the Professor arrives to help them with his knowledge of science. At first they are suspicious and point a gun at him, but he convinces them he is on their side.

The possessed zombies lay siege to the occupiers of the control room and try to persuade them to come out with various forms of persuasion.

This even includes playing music over the loud speakers, which enrages some of the workers further.

Quatermass says they should not listen to promises coming over the loud speakers. When three men ignore Quatermass and go out, they soon vanish from sight.

Meanwhile, Quatermass convinces the workers to pump pure oxygen to the pressure dome, theorising that it will drive the aliens into a desperate frenzy and eventually kill them, since oxygen is not a component of their planet's atmosphere.

Suddenly the pressure builds up and they are forced to cut the pipe. Blood drips from it when they open it up.

The Professor realises in horror that the aliens have blocked the oxygen flow to the pressure dome by stuffing the pipe with the pulped bodies of the men who went out to talk!

The workers are so enraged at this that they blast the pressure dome with a rocket launcher.

Lethal clouds of ammonia gas pour out, flooding the entire plant, and kill workers and zombies alike.

Only Quatermass survives, thanks to his gas mask.

Meanwhile, Dr Pugh has raced down to the plant in his car to help, only to run into the gas cloud. Quatermass finds him in the car, in a semi conscious state and they escape together.

Back at the rocket base, Quatermass wants to get ready to launch the Q2 rocket into space, as he realises the destruction of the planet has accomplished nothing in the fight against the alien menace.

But the base is over run by soldiers a few moments later. They are led by Captain John Dillon, who has returned, now under alien control.

Behind the Scenes

Jack Kine and Bernard Wilkie were the special effects department at the BBC's only two employees at the time of Quatermass 2. On Quatermass Experiment, Nigel Kneale himself had done the visual effect of the monster in Westminster Abbey. But the script for Q2 required more effects and now Kneale had Kine and Wilkie to realise the effects needed for the production.

To say Kine and Wilkie had to accomplish effects on a shoe string budget is something of an understatement. To illustrate this point, we might consider their experiences on Kneale and Cartier's production of Orwell's 1984.

The story goes that the amount of money the two men were given to do the effects for what was a major and prestigious production was so small that it included bus fare to the local hardware store and back and enough money to spend at that hardware store to purchase things they could use to mock up some futuristic props.

Their most impressive visual achievement was a communications device on the wall of the set which involved a single light which moved around in a circle. This was driven by a wind-up mechanism and Kine and Wilkie had to literally run around behind the set and wind up the mechanisms by hand when a scene was ready to be broadcast during the live transmission.

The total effects budget for 1984 was reportedly around fifty UK pounds, which was not small in the period but laughable compared to the multi million dollar effects budgets which were commonplace in film and television by the 1970s.

No doubt Quatermass 2 required another bus ride to the hardware store for Wilkie and Kine as they acquired some paint and some materials to build models. Quatermass Experiment had only shown a model rocket on Quatermass's desk, but this time around, the serial would feature actual miniature effects sequences.

One of the most impressive moments in the serial is the destruction of the pressure dome by rocket launcher blast. To do this effect, Kine and Wilkie submerged a dome inside a fish tank full of water.

When the actor in the live studio aimed the rocket launcher out the window and fired, the camera switched over to a close up of the model pressure dome. Kine and Wilkie caused the dome to rupture and split open in time for the camera.

Packed inside the dome was a mixture of paint and milk. If you've ever tipped some coffee into a sink of water, you will have noticed the way a colored liquid will slowly spill out and form a cloud in the water. Sure enough, a white cloud of what looks like smoke and gasses billowed out of the hole in the model dome, rising upwards towards the top of the tank.

The effect was similar to filming an explosion in slow motion. The vision soon switches to another shot. This time it is a shot of the full model of the plant. Kine and Wilkie had flooded the model with a cloud of white mist, produced with dry ice.

The impression given is that the gasses which had been contained in the pressure dome are now free to flood the plant, with lethal results. Upon cutting back to live action, we see filmed material of a zombie guard collapsing and dying from the gasses.

Combined with Clifford Hatts ' superb split-level set for the control room, the effects work help this episode work as tense drama in one location.

Review

The Frenzy is the very birth of the "Base Under Siege " formula of science fiction story which became a stape of mid 60s Doctor Who and much more besides.

This episode is the first time we see a small group of people, trapped in the control room of a high tech complex, under siege from alien-possessed killers.

As a result, it stand as one of the most influential episodes of television ever made.

The serial as a whole had far reaching influences on Doctor Who, UFO and The X Files, to name but three major examples, but this one episode is a real corker.

Tense, horrifying and compelling, this episode is virtually a climax for the the whole story in and of itself.

So much so that it was used as the ending for the later Hammer film version, which the events of the subsequent episode reduced to a mere aside.

Such Doctor Who serials as The Tenth Planet, The Moonbase, The Macra Terror, practically all of season five and and such later stories as

Earthshock owe much to the base under siege concept first presented here in this gripping episode of Quatermass 2.

Episode Six:

The Destroyers

The Destroyers begins was a rousing recap of the story to this point and we join Quatermass and his daughter at the rocket group as John Dillon announces that he and his men have the rocket base under their control.

However when Dillon enters, Dr Leo Pugh confronts him, but not before the Professor gets out one of his best monologues about the potential fate of the human race under the control of the aliens, describing the future for we humans as that of a subject species, feeding and serving the aliens, until they are brought to an end, choked to death perhaps in a changing atmosphere.

Pugh manages to get through to Dillon. Or does he? It seems rather too easy that Dillon should stand down his troops so willingly. Medical checks are done on Quatermass and Pugh and soon the Professor and the doctor prepare to take off in the Quatermas 2 rocket to rendezvous with the objective, as they call it, meaning the asteroid which is the source of meteorites.

The Professor intends to use the dangerously unstable nuclear power of his rocket motor, the same as the one which exploded in the desert of Northern Australia, as an offensive weapon to blow up the aliens asteroid.

Quatermass and gets one of his wittiest lines from Nigel Kneale as he refers to the rocket motor as an expensive and explosive dud and goes on to say that by using it against the aliens, which are a threat to the world, he may yet be able to give the tax payers some value for their money!

The rocket takes off, launching into the heavens, with the help of a ground based rocket technician (future Doctor Who guest Cyril Shaps, who graced such serials as Tomb of the Cybermen and Planet of the Spiders with his talents).

On the way Quatermass laments the fact that this flight should have been a great moment, a chance for brave young men to go heroically blasting through the heavens, but instead it's two old men on a kamikaze flight, not the way he would wanted it.

He he also discovers that Leo has brought along some added weight without consulting him. It's machine gun!

On the way to the asteroid Quatermass begins to see strange behaviour from his friend Leo Leo begins to have a flashback remembering his childhood days is a mathematical prodigy in a village school talking to his teacher who told him that is mathematical ability would give him the power to benefit mankind Quatermass confronts Leo and demands to know if the alien invaders have taken over his mind like all the others he met at the plant in Winnerden Flats.

The Professor puts forward the idea that when the alien force encounters a very complex human brain like Leo 's, maybe it takes longer to get control, but maybe the effect is deeper and more complete.

Sure enough, when the rocket crashes on the surface of the asteroid, Pugh dons his space helmet goes out.

Quatermass goes looking for him and the two spacewalking astronauts confront each other on the surface of the asteroid.

It's now clear why Dillon listened to what Leo Pugh had to say for he is indeed an agent of the aliens.

Deep inside the asteroid are the Amonids and it seems from Pugh's words that they wanted him to bring his rocket here because they intend to use it to take many more of their own kind back down to the Earth.

Suddenly, a number of slimy tendrils rise up out of the surface of the asteroid and ensnare the Quatermass 2 rocket.

Leo takes aim with the machine gun to kill Quatermass but when he fires the recoil blasts in backwards off the asteroid and sends him spinning away helplessly into space.

As Leo cries out for help, Quatermass boards the rocket and begins the nuclear reaction which will cause the engine to explode and then jettisons himself in the nosecone, flying off into space.

Behind him, the nuclear engine detonates, destroying the asteroid in a huge explosion.

Quatermass reports to ground control that it's over and on Earth Dillon is now free of alien control. Quatermass glance sadly at the empty seat where his friend Leo once sat.

He has succeeded and survived, but he is going home by himself. It seems Leo Pugh has died in space. As the rocket heads for home the end credits roll of Quatermass 2's final installment.

Behind the Scenes:

This is the most special effects-heavy episode of the serial but some behind the scenes factors involved the live action too. The space suits are a notable feature of the episode and the actors seem to struggle with them. The suits are segmented and tied together with twine.

At one point Jack Kine and Barnard Wilkie appear on screen assisting an actor getting into position, possibly caught late getting him ready in his suit.

John Robinson, struggling to hug Paula in the bulky space suit, has one of his best lines, "damn this thing! " He and Hugh Griffiths also seem to struggle in their seats and with the helmets during their take off sequence. At one point, when Quatermass gets up, the camera seems to catch him re-tying the twine that holds his space suit together.

There is a set for the surface of the asteroid, too, upon which Quatermass and Pugh go space walking.

This set is simple but effective enough on a low resolution screen, being made of tarps and blankets, draped carefully over boxes and bags, to create the look of a hilly, rocky, uneven piece of terrain.

The effects work was a big challenge for the ever resourceful and creative Kine and Wilkie. Having blown up the alien complex in the last episode, they now had to launch the Quatermass 2 rocket into space, land it on a rocky asteroid and blow it up.

The rocket launch was done by using one of the oldest techniques of stage magic, operating objects which are brightly lit, by using sticks and rods painted black, against a totally black backdrop.

As smoke pours from their model rocket, it is lifted skyward by a black rod or stick attached to the back of the rocket. A second shot shows it curving toward the backdrop, but this works as it looks like the camera is tilting to follow it, showing the underside as the rocket rises towards space.

The rod is invisible against a black bad drop, but it casts a shadow in the smoke clouds. However, this could easily be a shadow from some part of a gantry and does not shatter the illusion.

Their effects work struggles with the stage separation in space and the scene of Leo Pugh spinning away into space, the wires and a shadow of the model astronaut visible against the space backdrop.

However, they do very well with running the film backwards to show strands of creepy, slimy Amonid tentacle rising up out of the asteroid surface to wrap around the hull of Quatermass' rocket.

With a mere pittance to spend of the effects, Kine and Wilkie's inventiveness and creativity really wins through in Q2, making the serial enjoyable in a way that is very much reminiscent of early Dr Who, a show Bernard Wilkie would go on to work for.

Colony in Space features some impressive color effective from Wilkie, showing the planet Uxarius appearing through the colorful swirling lights of the space-time vortex.

Possibly one of the most ironic moments on 70s Dr Who was when an image of Jack Kine, possibly a staff photograph from the BBC files, was used as the face of a Big Brother style dictator in the serial Inferno, in which the Doctor finds himself in England in a parallel world where the country has become an Orwellian dictatorship, probably inspired by Kneale's 1984.

Matt Irvine would later create a sequence for the Dr Who serial The Invisible Enemy which looks a lot like a remake of the sequence in which Quatermass sees alien life growing inside the pressure dome.

The similarity of this sequence, probably a direct homage, led to some UK fans speculating that plans were afoot to remake Quatermass 2 but to date there has been no confirmed plan by the BBC to remake Q2.

Review

Despite the shift away from gritty horror and Earth bound realism to early space opera and adventures in orbit, the episode succeeds on a number of levels, even though it is a mixed bag of results for the visual effects department.

John Robinson in particular has a great week with his acting, getting some lengthy dramatic speeches and a couple of funny lines, which he delivers with real skill and passion.

Certainly his reaction to the loss of Dr Leo Pugh at the very end is quite touching.

The ending is generally great, although as the rocket capsule sputters away into space, smoke streaming behind it, some viewers were left wondering about the fate of the brave Professor, since we do not see him return to Earth.

This indicates Quatermass had begun the era of weekly TV and viewers would have liked to have seen more episodes after episode six, to see

Quatermass return home and find out what happens next. Unfortunately, Quatermass would not return until two years later and played by a different actor and without any word on the fate or lives of his daughter or Dillon.

Nevertheless, had John Robinson failed, as Quatermass, then there would never have been a Quatermass and the Pit. Quatermass 2 and Robinson succeeded admirably and the ratings were enormous.

In fact, with many more people owning television than ther had been in 1953, Quatermass 2 was viewed by many people who would have heard about the fuss around Quatermass Experiment but would have felt that they had missed out because they did own a television yet.

Kneale cemedted Quatermass with his second serial and John Robinson saved the day by stepping into the breach following Reginald Tate's untimely demise.

Robinson deserves praise for what he accomplished. It is due to him that Quatermass 2 succeeded, despite the death of Reginald Tate, and the name Quatermass continued to be held in high regard as an audience grabber.

Main Cast and Crew Credits:

Created, Narrated and Written by Nigel Kneale

Starring John Robinson as Professor Bernard Quatermass

Monica Grey as Paula

Hugh Griffith as Dr Leo Pugh

John Stone as Captain John Dillon

Opening theme   "Mars, Bringer of War" by Gustav Holst

Country of origin   United Kingdom

No. of episodes   6

Production

Producer(s)   Rudolph Cartier Danny Bowie

Directed by Rudolph Cartier

Camera setup: Multi-camera (film on location, video tape in studio)

Running time   Approx. 30 mins per episode (over-running was common)

Release

Original network   BBC

Picture format   405-line black-and-white

Original release   22 October – 26 November 1955

Also released on DVD with the surviving episodes of Quatermas Experiment and the complete series of Quatermass and the Pit.

The Quatermass 2 movie from Hammer Films.

American actor Brian Donlevy returns and becomes the only actor to play Quatermass twice in the series. The Hammer produced movie of Quatermass Two was different to the movie of Quatermass Xperiment in one significant way in that Nigel Kneale was invited to co-write the script with director Val Guest this time.

Although Brian Donleavy reprises his role as the movie version of Professor Quatermass, some have noted that the word professor is not used in the movie at all. Instead he is simply referred to by his distinctive surname.

Val Guest directs the script with the same movie-reel style and documentary-like realism that he brought to the previous film but the fact that this is a follow-up makes it only better because the experience shows and everyone delivers a superior product compared to the first film. (And since Quatermass Xperiment was something of a small masterpiece itself, this is quite an accomplishment).

Although critics gave the movie a mixed response at the time, it is regarded by many viewers and critics nowadays as one of the greatest British science fiction films ever made and possibly the most realistic and convincing alien invasion story ever told in a movie.

Kneale had disliked the casting of a brusque American in the first film and was just as unhappy with Donlevy once again. He felt Donlevy played the good Professor like a motor mechanic and had little grasp of technical dialog, in stark contrast to Guest, who cast him happily, in the belief that his down to Earth and no-nonsense style added a level of believability to the whole affair.

Kneale was on record as saying that he was unhappy with the Val Guest movies overall, preferring his TV plays as the real deal, the genuine items.

However American director Joe Dante has said that he met Nigel Kneale and told him that he felt his opinion was wrong. He told Kneale that he was lucky to have someone like Val Guest make such great, high-quality, well-made movies of his stories so that these great stories would be kept alive for the future generations to discover and enjoy.

Quatermass 2 kicks off in a very different way on the big screen compared to the TV version.

Quatermass is run off the road by a car driven by woman who is desperate to get her male partner to hospital for medical attention in the opening hook, shown as a pre-credits sequence to get the audience involved fast. His face has been burned by a terrible mark by a mysterious stone.

As they try to move the car, Quatermass and the woman see the man with the mark suddenly get up and run off like a madman. This event leads to his realising something is wrong when technicians at his rocket base detect meteorites falling in the area the woman had come from, Winnerden Flats.

He film features two characters from Quatermass Xperiment who were not in the TV version of Q2, Inspector Lomax and Marsh, although both are recast here. Future Carry On legend Sid James plays a reporter who is loosely developed from James Fullalove, who was also in Quatermass Experiment but not in Q2. (He would return for the TV version of The Pit, but not the Hammer movie version, oddly enough.)

The score for the film is outstanding and creepy and the film features some impressive visuals for special effects for the film work courtesy of Les Bowie, a man who would eventually won an Oscar as part of the special effects team on Superman the Movie in the late 1970s.

Bowie's specialty was in matte paintings and clever visual compositions and almost every special effect in the movie is at painting done by Les Bowie, from the complex at Winnerden flats, to the giant pressure domes which Quatermass runs away from, to the rocket which stands on a platform behind Quatermass when he arrives at the rocket base.

All of these images are done by Les Bowie as Matt paintings. In other words he painted the rocket or the pressure dome or the Winnerden Flats complex itself onto a sheet of glass, which was then slotted into a frame in front of the lens of the film camera. When the camera was lined up perfectly so that the painted image appeared to be part of the overall picture the camera was looking at, the effects are absolutely superb, much like modern CG enhancements, albeit static.

Although there are only a few of them, they are all extremely convincing. There is one unusual special effect shot at the end of the film when the Quatermass 2 rocket is launched.

In the movie it is launched without a crew, in a short scene, while Quatermass is involved in the siege. We see the base of a rocket with sparks coming out of it, lifting up.

This appears to be one quick model shot. The interesting thing about the effect is that it is composited into a kind of window or observation viewport and the camera is made to shake so that the entire room seems to be rocking violently like in an earthquake for a few moments, while the rocket itself remains perfectly still and blasts off.

This effect is quite a good illusion of a rocket launch.

Another interesting special effect is a shot of the rocket exploding in space. This appears to have been achieved firstly by projecting stars, probably with a slide projector, onto a white cloth. The explosion seems to be caused by a spotlight aimed at the back of the cloth. When the spotlight was switched on, it caused a circle of light to appear in "space " and spread out, filling up most of the screen.

There is also some extensive use of miniature effects for the finale in which the blob-like alien monsters burst out of the pressure dome and go rampaging through their Earth base before dying and collapsing and burning up.

It does appear that actors were inside the blobs walking around on a model set, although is not documented.

Extensive pyrotechnics seem to have been employed for the explosions and the subsequent burning of the blob-like monsters and a wind machine similar to a propeller-driven aeroplane engine was used to generate the incredible wind in the finale caused by the destruction of the complex .

This apparently caused the hairpiece worn by Brian Donlevy to fly off.

Once again it was noted by the director that the Donlevy drank continually during the production but it did not seem to impede or affect his acting performance.

Donlevy himself is far better in this film and he was in the first. Although he was effectively driven, determined and single-minded in the first movie, we see a much more thoughtful, compassionate and sympathetic hero in this movie.

Donlevy does well throughout the film and has many fans in spite of the criticisms he received from Nigel Kneale and from some Quatermass fans who felt that the good professor should have been played only by an Englishman and portrayed as a sensitive and thoughtful intellectual.

Val guests direction is exceptionally good from start to finish.

It's a pity we don't get to see Quatermass go up into space and go spacewalking like on the TV version, of course.

However using the rocket as an unmanned missile to destroy the asteroid is a simple yet effective variation on the plot.

The climactic base under siege storyline in which everyone is trapped in the pressure control room at the complex is very well done in the movie version, recapturing everything which made The Frenzy such a great installment.

The site of the gargantuan Amonid monsters bursting out and rampaging through the refinery manages to give the film a big scale, impressive finale which is just as enjoyable in its own way as its TV counterpart.

Overall Quatermass 2is a great movie and as an early work of alien invasion conspiracy storytelling it remains a film which stands the test of time.

It is a true great from Hammer films, mirroring the paranoia and distrust of government which permeated the Cold War era.

Joe Dante was right when he said Nigel Kneale was wrong to reject these movies because Val Guest and Brian Donlevy delivered a superb film to keep this great story alive for future generations to enjoy and made Quatermass an international phenomenon, not just a British one.

According to Wikipedia and the Internet Movie Data Base, "The film was originally shot in Ansco Color, developed by Agfa, but released in black-and-white. The colour negative still exists in the archives. "

However, this claim that it was shot in color is almost certainly not true. It appears to be another urban myth, like the Q2 remake floated by Dr Who fans after The Invisible Enemy was aired.

In this case, the culprit is probably a fan made website featuring colorised still from the movie and a number of wildly implausible fake "quotes " attributed to people involved in the making of the movie.

Quatermass 2 Movie Credits:

Directed by Val Guest

Produced by Anthony Hinds

Screenplay by Nigel Kneale and Val Guest

Based on The Quatermass 2 TV series 1955

by Nigel Kneale

Starring:

Brian Donlevy as Quatermass

With

John Longden

Sid James

Bryan Forbes

William Franklyn

Vera Day

Music by James Bernard

Cinematography   Gerald Gibbs

Edited by   James Needs

Production

company

Hammer Film Productions

Distributed by Exclusive Films (UK), United Artists (USA)

Release date

   24 May 1957

Running time

85 minutes

Country United Kingdom

Language English

Budget £92,000

Influence on Subsequent Television Series.

Dr Who.

Perhaps the most obvious and extensive borrowing of elements from this story to appear in Doctor Who was in the serial Spearhead from Space. Starring Jon Pertwee in his debut, the plot is so close to Quatermass 2 it could almost be a color remake. Robert Holmes adds some of his own touches, such as animated window dummies instead of possessed humans, but plot wise, the hollow meteorites and their concealed intelligences, as well as the factory with an alien in a tank, are all there!

The factory setting and people in authority under alien influence had been used before this, however, for The Invasion, a story featuring the Cybermen.

Inhuman people who turn out to be replicants or robots would again feature in the Tom Baker story The Android Invasion and the Peter Davison story Resurrection of the Daleks.

While both owe much to Invasion of the Body Snatchers, there is plenty of Quatermass element in both. Android Invasion features an astronaut returning from a space mission and a British Space Defence complex.

Resurrection has an army bomb disposal squad investigating alien objects, discovered by builders, who thought they were unexploded bombs, a nod to Quatermass and the Pit. The bomb squad are soon replaced by dehumanised killer copies.

UFO.

Gerry and Sylvia Anderson's amazing first live-action SF series, UFO, starred Ed Bishop as the head of a secret government organization at war with aliens from a dying planet. Featuring a high budget and great visual effects, the series also was deeply paranoid Cold War era science fiction drama.

Many episodes feature humans controlled by aliens or plots to cover up the existence of aliens for the sake of government security.

ESP, for example, features a telepathic man falling under alien control, used as a killer, his mission to assassinate Ed Bishop's Straker character.

The Square Triangle asks challenging moral questions about the government covering up the truth about UFOs. A woman and her lover plot to murder her husband, but when they kill an alien by accident, Straker wipes their memories. But will the murder now proceed?

But perhaps the most Quatermass style episode of all is The Man Who Came Back, in which an astronaut goes missing in space, later returning under alien control. At the end of the episode, Ed Bishop's Straker and the possessed man take a space walk and end up fighting to the death in space, an ending very reminiscent of the Quatermass and Pugh showdown in space from The Destroyers.

The X Files.

Possibly the most paranoid series ever made, rivaled only by The Prisoner, X-Files focused on two FBI Agents, Mulder and Scully, and their quest to uncover the truth about UFOs, concealed by a government conspiracy.

At the height of its popularity, the X-Files became a movie with Fight the Future. With a supporting appearance by Martin Landau, Fight the Future was a good movie, but many noted that it was so close to Quatermass 2 and Quatermass and the Pit in plot details, some were saying Nigel Kneale should have been given a credit for writing.

Featuring a black oil or black slime which was much like the synthetic food from Winnerden flats, X-Files and the movie seemed to be taking elements of Quatermass and making them part of a longer running series.

The success and popularity of X Files was just one more example of the lasting power of Nigel Kneake's ideas.

Quatermass

and

the Pit

The Plot of Quatermass and the Pit.

London, 1957. Workmen discover a pre-human skull while building in the fictional Hobbs Lane (formerly Hob's Lane, Hob being an antiquated name for the Devil) in Knightsbridge, London. Dr Matthew Roney, paleontologist, examines the remains and reconstructs a dwarf-like humanoid with a large brain capacity which he believes to be a primitive man. As further excavation is undertaken, something that looks like a missile is unearthed; further work by Roney's group is halted because the military believe it to be an unexploded Second World War bomb.

Roney calls in his friend Professor Bernard Quatermass of the British Rocket Group to prevent the military from disturbing what he believes to be an archaeological find. Quatermass and Colonel Breen, recently appointed to lead the Rocket Group over Quatermass's objections, become intrigued by the site. As more of the artefact is uncovered additional fossils are found, which Roney dates to five million years, suggesting that the object is at least that old. The interior is empty, and a symbol of five intersecting circles, which Roney identifies as the occult pentacle, is etched on a wall that appears to conceal an inner chamber.

The shell of the object is so hard that even a boron nitride drill makes no impression, and when the attempt is made, vibrations cause severe distress in people around the object. Quatermass interviews local residents and discovers ghosts and poltergeists have been common in the area for decades. A hysterical soldier is carried out of the object, claiming to have seen a dwarf-like apparition walk through the wall of the artefact, a description that matches a 1927 newspaper account of a ghost.

Following the drilling, a hole opens up in the object's interior wall. Inside, Quatermass and the others find the remains of insect-like aliens resembling giant three-legged locusts, with stubby antennae on their heads giving the impression of horns. As Quatermass and Roney examine the remains, they theorise the aliens may have come from a planet habitable five million years ago – Mars.

While clearing his equipment from the craft the drill operator triggers more poltergeist activity, and runs through the streets in a panic until he finds sanctuary in a church. Quatermass and Roney find him there, and he describes visions of the insect aliens killing each other. As Quatermass investigates the history of the area, he finds accounts dating back to medieval times about devils and ghosts, all centred on incidents where the ground was disturbed. He suspects a psychic projection of these beings has remained on the alien ship and is being seen by those who come into contact with it.

Quatermass decides to use Roney's optic-encephalogram, a device that records impressions from the optical centres of the brain, and see the visions for himself. Roney's assistant, Barbara Judd, is most sensitive; placing the device on her, they record a violent purge of the Martian hive to root out unwanted mutations. Quatermass concludes that in its most primitive phase mankind was visited by this race of Martians. Some apes and primitive pre-humans were taken away and genetically altered to give them abilities such as telepathy, telekinesis and other psychic powers. They were then returned to Earth, and the buried artefact is one of the ships that had crashed at the end of its journey. With their home world dying, the aliens had tried to change humanity's ancestors to have minds and abilities similar to their own, but with a bodily form adapted to life on Earth.

But the aliens became extinct before completing their work. As the human race bred and evolved, only a percentage retained their psychic abilities, which surfaced only sporadically. For centuries the buried ship had occasionally triggered those dormant abilities, which explained the reports of poltergeists; people were unknowingly using their own telekinesis to move objects around, and the ghost sightings were traces of a racial memory. The authorities, and Breen in particular, find this explanation preposterous despite being shown the recording of Barbara's vision. They believe that the craft is a Nazi propaganda weapon and the alien bodies fakes designed to create exactly the impressions that Quatermass has succumbed to, and decide to hold a media event to stem the rumours that are already spreading.

Quatermass warns that if implanted psychic powers survive in the human race, there could also still be an ingrained compulsion to enact the "Wild Hunt" of a race purge, but the media event goes ahead regardless. The power cables that string into the craft fully activate it for the first time, and glowing and humming like a living thing it starts to draw upon this energy source and awaken the ancient racial programming. Those Londoners in whom the alien admixture remains strong fall under the ship's influence; they merge into a group mind and begin a telekinetic mass murder of those without the alien genes, an ethnic cleansing of those the alien race mind considers to be impure and weak.

Breen stands transfixed and is eventually consumed by the energies from the craft as it slowly melts away and an image of a Martian "devil" floats in the sky above London. Fires and riots erupt, and after Quatermass succumbs to the mass psychosis he attempts to kill Roney, who does not have the alien gene and is therefore immune to the alien influence. Roney manages to shake Quatermass out of his trance, and remembering the legends of demons and their aversion to iron and water, he proposes that a sufficient mass of iron connected to wet earth may be sufficient to short-circuit the apparition. Quatermass acquires a length of iron chain and tries to reach the "devil" but succumbs to its psychic pressure. Roney manages to walk up to the apparition and hurls the chain at it, resulting in him and the spacecraft being reduced to ashes.

At the conclusion of the final episode Quatermass, apparently talking live on the BBC to the public about the events which have taken place, delivers a warning directly to camera: "We are the Martians! If we cannot control the inheritance within us, this will be their second dead planet."

(Synopsis courtesy of Wikipedia).

Comments:

By the year 1957, scientists in popular culture were undergoing something of a change in the way they were portrayed. It was during the Second World War scientists became very prominent as the experts who could develop super weapons capable of saving the world from fascism as represented by Hitler and the Nazis.

Werner Von Braun, the rocketry expert, had been suborned by Hitler to develop the V two rockets which had been used in attacks on London during the Blitz.

And Albert Einstein had been another world famous and potent scientific figure with his famous special theory of relativity making him a household name. Oppenheimer and the development of the atomic bomb had made scientists terrifying as well as towering authorities. The public knew scientists could come up with weapons capable of destroying the world and this was a source of fear, the type of fear that sat beneath civilization, like an undercurrent of unease.

On the other hand, there were astronomers such as Bernard Lovell and others who took a more benevolent and humanistic role in popular culture. The name Bernard was in fact taken from Lovell and used by Nigel Kneale for his scientist hero.

In his first outing, Quatemass was a rocket scientist and pioneer and also a compassionate humanist.

His encounter with an alien life form which had taken possession of his astronauts during a test flight into space forced the Professor to become a modern day Van Helsing.

Just as Van Helsing was the expert and enemy of the vampire Dracula ,Quatermass was the scientific expert and enemy of monsters from space possessing human bodies.

In his second outing, the Professor went beyond being just a modern Van Helsing.

He became more of a detective and investigator as well as a scientist, uncovering alien evils hidden among us.

Just as Sherlock Holmes used forensic science in solving crimes, Quatermass uses his knowledge of space science to track down and expose an alien conspiracy to infiltrate the British government and take over the world in Quatermass 2. The idea of the scientist as the all-purpose hero for fighting aliens and monsters, or indeed the all-purpose mad genius villain who is out to destroy the world, was soon widespread in film and television.

By 1957, it was becoming apparent that it was time for the all knowing scientist to have his scientific knowledge sorely tested by forces which reminded him of the old adage that there are, in the words of Shakespeare's Hamlet, *more things in Heaven and Earth than are dreamed of in your philosophy.*

Quatermass and the Pit was a big break away from what are gone before in the Quatermass series. In this third serial the professor is forced to face up to things which he does not believe are possible.

The professor is faced with a haunted house and stories of ghosts. He is faced with legends of imps and Demons and foul noises sent from Hell by the Devil himself. At first the professor is completely sceptical about these things too. As a man of science, he rejects notions of ghosts and the supernatural. But as the story progresses, forensic evidence and historical records and eyewitness accounts gradually force him to open his mind to the possibility that there are things far beyond his scientific knowledge.

The evidence of something evil is in fact all around, the evidence surrounds us all in our everyday world. Quatermass notices the name of "Hobb's Lane " is different to the far older name plate which reads "Hob's Lane " and we learn that Hob was a nickname for the Devil. Satan was often referred to politely as Robin Goodfellow and demons were often called Hobgoblins.

Quatermass must consult written records at the Westminster Abbey archives to learn about the past, about accounts of people claiming to struggle against evil and afflictions sent from Hell.

The scientist Quatermass is faced with the idea that his bland assumptions of scientific certainty are mistaken and have initially blinded him to far stranger possibilities, things he cannot readily explain away.

This idea of meta science or things which lie beyond the knowledge and comprehension science is at the heart of Quatermass and the Pit and by the end of the story the professor is faced with an image of the face of Satan himself, risen and hovering over London, implacable yet baleful and deadly.

As with Kneale's later television play The Stone Tape, which suggests the past can be recorded or stored in the very stones of the Earth, Quatermass and the Pit dramatises a clash between science and the supernatural, with unnerving results.

Kneale's response to this notion of a scientist facing myths and legends which all but shatter his cosy convictions is to suggest that science can find some kind of logical explanation in the end, just not one which disproves the existence of ghosts and Demons, only one which rationalises them as real in some kind of logical way.

While the idea of supernatural forces and haunted houses seems implausible at first, it is written and printed records of the past and interviewing a deeply disturbed witness which helps him to finally accept how misplaced his smug scepticism has been. This investigative approach, like a kind of supernatural detective probe, gradually uncovers enough to convince the skeptical man of science to take the supernatural threat seriously.

And when it turns out to be aliens who have generated these seemingly supernatural forces, the serial is no less potent when it suggests that racism and prejudice have been hardwired into human DNA by the Martians along with the old powers. As a TV event, Quatermass and the Pit is both persuasive and a drama with a direct message. We need to control our own bad tendencies and learn to live in peace together or we will destroy ourselves.

The Hammer movie of this serial, the only one made in color, is outstanding and remarkably faithful to the TV original. If the scenes of Quatermass clashing with Colonel Breen seem familiar to fans of Doctor Who, their relationship was almost certainly the inspiration for the Doctor's relationship with Brigadier Lethbridge-Stewart, clashing over the scientific and the military attitudes to alien incidents.

Main Cast of Quatermass and the Pit.

André Morell as Quatermass

Cec Linder as Dr Roney

Anthony Bushell as Colonel Breen

Christine Finn as Barbara Judd

Written by Nigel Kneale

Directed by Rudolph Cartier

The Quatermass Conclusion.

Plot:

In the last quarter of the 20th century, the whole world seemed to sicken. Civilised institutions, whether old or new, fell ... as if some primal disorder was reasserting itself. And men asked themselves, "Why should this be?"

— Opening narration (spoken by Gurov), Quatermass, Chapter One: Ringstone Round by Nigel Kneale.

Chapter One: Ringstone Round

Quatermass (John Mills), now living in retirement in Scotland, travels to London in search of his granddaughter, Hettie Carlson (Rebecca Saire), who has gone missing. He is shocked by the scale of the urban collapse that has struck the city – law and order has broken down and marauding gangs terrorise the litter-strewn, decaying streets. The fall of civilization has been general across the world. Appearing as a guest on a television programme covering the "Hands in Space" project, a joint space mission between the United States and Russia, Quatermass is horrified when the two spacecraft are destroyed by some unknown force. Astronomer Joe Kapp (Simon MacCorkindale), another guest on the programme, invites Quatermass to join him at his home in the country where he and two friends have constructed two radio telescopes. At the radio telescope site, Kapp's colleagues report that they detected a powerful signal at the exact time of the incident in space. Quatermass is intrigued by the behaviour of a group of hippie-like youngsters known as the Planet People, who are travelling to various neolithic sites (about 5,000 years old) from where they believe they will be transported to a better life on another planet. Quatermass suspects Hettie has joined them. Along with Kapp's wife, Claire (Barbara Kellerman), Quatermass and Kapp follow a group of Planet People to a stone circle of megaliths, Ringstone Round. As they watch, the Planet People assembled inside the circle are bathed in a bright light and disappear, leaving only a residue of white dust behind.

Chapter Two: Lovely Lightning

The Planet People's leader, Kickalong (Ralph Arliss), believes that the Planet People gathered at Ringstone Round have been transported—as promised—to "the planet", but it is clear to Quatermass and Kapp that they have been reduced to ashes. One badly burnt survivor – a girl called Isabel (Annabelle Lanyon) who deliriously talks about "lovely lightning" – is found and is brought back to the Kapps' cottage. Making contact with NASA scientist Chuck Marshall (Tony Sibbald), they learn that thousands of young people have disappeared in similar incidents at similar sites all around the world. Quatermass, aided by District Commissioner Annie Morgan (Margaret Tyzack), decides to bring Isabel to London for tests. As they make their journey, Quatermass speculates as to whether there is any connection between recent events and the decline in society. Reaching London, they are attacked by a gang. Quatermass is yanked from the car but Annie and Isabel manage to escape. Meanwhile, a large number of Planet People arrive at the radio telescope, congregating at the stone circle on its grounds. Working some distance away, Kapp is horrified to see the light strike the area where his home is and rushing home, he finds his family gone as it was caught in the radius of the deadly light. His two friends and dog died too.

Chapter Three: What Lies Beneath

Quatermass is rescued by a group of elderly people living in a scrap yard who doctor his injuries. At the hospital, the doctors are shocked when Isabel levitates off her bed and explodes in a cloud of dust. Elsewhere, the devastated Kapp is left alone in the ruins of his cottage and observatory. More and more young people are joining the Planet People, including the gangs that have been terrorising the cities and the soldiers assigned to keep them away from the Megalithic sites. Contact is restored with Chuck Marshall and with the Russians in the form of Gurov (Brewster Mason).

Quatermass theorises that this is not the first time this has happened; megalithic sites such as prehistoric stone circles are in fact markers where beacons have been left by the people living then as a sign that something terrible happened there, and that there are some kind of alien markers buried underground at these sites. Quatermass believes there is a sphere of energy surrounding the Earth. The Russians and the Americans send a space shuttle, commanded by Marshall, to make contact with the force. Quatermass is sceptical; he believes they are dealing not with an intelligence but with a machine constructed to harvest human protein. The space shuttle reports a giant beam of light stretching from somewhere in deep space to the Earth, just missing them. A second beam just afterwards destroys them. Meanwhile, the Planet People are gathering at Wembley Stadium in the tens of thousands. Annie and Quatermass travel to the stadium but are powerless to prevent the Planet People from gathering. When they are attacked, Annie drives their car into the underground car park beneath the stadium where she crashes the vehicle and is killed. The lightning strikes the stadium and Quatermass underground, huddles against the wall to try and survive.

Chapter Four: An Endangered Species

Quatermass showing signs of his recent narrow escape emerges from the car park to find the stadium empty. An estimated 70,000 people died there. So many have now been harvested that the particles of dust in the air have turned the sky green. Kapp attempts to repair his equipment in order to contact the alien presence, but the Planet People destroy his efforts. They try to persuade him to join them but he refuses, convinced now that his family are dead. Quatermass, aided by Gurov, who has travelled to London from Moscow, assembles a team of scientists to find a solution. He deliberately selects old people for the task as they are immune to the call of the alien force. Quatermass decides to set a trap. He plans to fake the presence of a gathering of a million young people at Kapp's observatory and, when the force comes, to detonate a 35 kiloton nuclear weapon. It is a focused charge where most of the force will go upwards, causing little damage in the area. Quatermass does not believe this will be sufficient to destroy the alien machine but he hopes that it will shock it enough to make it go away. Kapp volunteers to stay behind with Quatermass to help detonate the bomb. The pair set up the trap and wait in darkness. Suddenly, Kickalong appears with a group of Planet People, including Quatermass' granddaughter, Hettie. Kapp tries to warn them away but is shot and killed by Kickalong. The light appears, indicating that the alien force beam has arrived, but the shock of seeing his granddaughter among the Planet People causes Quatermass to suffer a heart attack. She has recognised him too and struggling to reach the detonator button, Quatermass is aided by Hettie and together they detonate the bomb. Later in a world that is recovering from the recent fall of civilization, Gurov tells us: "The message was taken. It has not come again. We pray it will never come again".

(synopsis courtesy of Wikipedia).

Quatermass Conclusion in Review:

Quatermass Conclusion arrived at the end of the 1970s and with a fair amount of attention and interest in the UK. In Australia, however, the four hour length episodes were joined into a mini-series of two two-hour installments. The reaction from many in the UK seems to have been disappointment, that after such anticipation, there were four one hour episodes and then the main character was killed off, like a weekly series that gets axed after just four weeks.

But in Australia, where there was no real anticipation, but people were used to mini series since the success of Alex Haley's Roots, Quatermass Conclusion, billed simply as Quatermass, made a strong impact.

The crumbling decay of western civilisation into a dystopian mess has become a cliche since 1979, but at the time it was a shock to see on screen and the theme of folk horror with ties to Stonehenge was fascinating.

Verity Lambert of Dr Who fame produced the mini series on film and made it look genuinely impressive. While Andre Morrell and Andrew Keir are generally regarded as the best Quatermass actors for their performances in the TV and film versions of Quatermass and the Pit, Sir John Mills manages to hold his own as an aged but still wise and clever Quatermass.

His search for his granddaughter is touching and Mills is vulnerable and strong in the right places.

The alien machine harvests people like an alien Grim Reaper, carrying out a fully automated extermination of masses of humans which echoes the Book of Revelation and the Nazi Death Camps in the Holocaust at the same time. The Jewish Joe Kapp sees his vulnerable wife, his beautiful sweet children and his warm home reduced to ashes in one of the cruelest moments in television history and Kapp declares it evil, rightfully so.

It takes the sacrifice of Quatermass ' life to stop the end of Mankind in the end of the story, but Kneale delivers one last moment of sheer storytelling genius when Quatermass comes face to face with his absent granddaughter at the last second and promptly has a fatal heart attack, echoing the real life death of original Quatermas actor Reginald Tate.

With her help, Quatermass presses the switch and it's all over. This time there was no cinema remake, but there was a compilation feature made and Kneale, knowing this was happening, wrote for it, with the result that the feature actually works really well in its own right. And so, with his final noble act, one of pop culture's greatest icons dies, only to live on in the 2005 Quatermass Experiment remake, the Quatermass Memoirs audio and whatever lies ahead for the famous Professor.

About the author.

Adrian Sherlock grew up in the city of Geelong, near Melbourne Australia and still lives there with his family. He teaches and writes and has had much involvement in theatre, film making, acting and directing.

He is also a dedicated fan of British popular culture, notably Dr. Who, Quatermass, Sapphire and Steel and the works of Gerry and Sylvia Anderson. With a surname like Sherlock he has been aware of Sherlock Holmes all his life.

When he was young, he became hooked on the Target Dr. Who novels written by people such as Terrance Dicks, David Whitaker, Ian Marter, Malcolm Hulke and John Peel. These books imparted a love of reading which led him to study literature and writing at University.

He is also a contributing writer to the "Lethbridge-Stewart" series of novels and short stories. His short story The Playing Dead is about a deserted town and zombies and his novel The New Unusual deals with a 70s craze for interacting with so called dream-eggs which bend minds. In both cases, alien menaces lurk in the background, as one might expect.

Made in the USA
Las Vegas, NV
24 January 2022

42230575R00049